D1164569

Published in 2013 by The Rosen Publishing Group, Inc.
29 East 21st Street, New York, NY 10010

Photo Credits: **KEY** tl=top left; tc=top center; tr=top right; cl=center left; c=center; cr=center right; bl=bottom left; bc=bottom center; br=bottom right; bg=background
CBT = Corbis; iS = istockphoto.com; SH = Shutterstock; TF = Topfoto; TPL = photolibrary.com
front cover bg, bg iS; **1**c SH; **2–3**bg TPL; **4–5**bg CBT; **6**c, cr CBT; tr SH; cl TF; **6–7**bg iS; **7**bl, br, tr TF; **8**bl TF; **8–9**bg TF; tc iS; **9**br, cr CBT; **10**tl CBT; **10–11**bg iS; **11**tr CBT; br SH; **12**bl SH; br TPL; **15**br, cr TF; **16**bc TF; **17**tc TF; **18**tl SH; bl, cr TF; **19**br TF; **22**tr iS; tr TF; **23**bl, br, tl, tr iS; bl, br, tl, tr TF; **24**c CBT; **25**tc TF; **26–27**cl TPL; **28**bl SH; c, tr TF; **28–29**bc TF; **29**bl, br, tl TF; cr TPL

All illustrations copyright Weldon Owen Pty Ltd. **7**tl; **10**bl; **12**tr; **17**bl; **19**tc; **27**bc Andrew Davies/Creative Communication

Weldon Owen Pty Ltd
Managing Director: Kay Scarlett
Creative Director: Sue Burk
Publisher: Helen Bateman
Senior Vice President, International Sales: Stuart Laurence
Vice President Sales North America: Ellen Towell
Administration Manager, International Sales: Kristine Ravn

Library of Congress Cataloging-in-Publication Data

Sheehan, Robert.
 Francis Drake: patriot or pirate? / by Robert Sheehan.
    p. cm. — (Discovery education: sensational true stories)
 Includes index.
 ISBN 978-1-4777-0060-0 (library binding) — ISBN 978-1-4777-0105-8 (pbk.) —
 ISBN 978-1-4777-0106-5 (6-pack)
 1. Drake, Francis, Sir, 1540?-1596—Juvenile literature. 2. Explorers—Great Britain—Biography—Juvenile literature. I. Title.
 DA86.22.D7S54 2013
 942.05'5092—dc23
 [B]
                                        2012019588

Manufactured in the United States of America

CPSIA Compliance Information: Batch #W13PK2: For Further Information contact Rosen Publishing, New York, New York at 1-800-237-9932

SENSATIONAL TRUE STORIES

FRANCIS DRAKE
PATRIOT OR PIRATE?
ROBERT SHEEHAN

PowerKiDS press.

New York

Contents

Adventurous Life

Francis Drake was born in Tavistock, England, in 1540. He learned sailing and navigating skills at the Plymouth home of his wealthy second cousin, John Hawkins, and probably began his sailing career at 22 years old.

Drake was a courageous and daring sea captain. He was a slave trader who also plundered the treasure of Spain, the world power of the era. He circumnavigated the globe and was made a knight of England. He was a leading naval commander in the great English victory over the Spanish navy, the Spanish Armada. The question remains: was he a patriot or a pirate?

1547
Plymouth is on the south coast of England. Francis Drake moved there at the age of seven to live with seafaring relatives and learn mariner skills.

1554
Mary I, Queen of England, married Philip II of Spain. Philip saw the marriage as a political alliance to build good relationships with England.

1567
Drake sailed with John Hawkins to the New World. Their ships were attacked by the Spanish at San Juan de Ulúa, in Mexico, and they only just escaped.

1572
With his crew, Drake mad a land attack on Nombre Dios, in Panama. They sto Spanish gold and silver th was intended for transpo to Spain.

77
ake set off on his first
cumnavigation of the
obe. He sailed via the
ait of Magellan, around
e tip of South America
d into the Pacific Ocean.

1586
Drake captured Santo
Domingo in the Dominican
Republic, as well as other
Spanish settlements in the
Caribbean. This led Spain to
plot war against England.

1587
The Spanish fort at Cádiz, in
Spain, was equipped with
cannons. Drake entered the
harbor, took the Spanish
by surprise, and destroyed
almost 40 ships.

1596
Sir Francis Drake died of
dysentery while at sea,
off the coast of Panama.
This statue of Sir Francis,
with a sword and globe,
stands in Plymouth.

The Times

Sixteenth-century Europe was a turbulent place. Spain was the dominant and wealthiest world power, with colonies in the New World. England was small and insignificant. Henry VII of England began the English Tudor dynasty in 1485. It lasted until the death of his granddaughter, Queen Elizabeth I, in 1603.

Francis Drake was 18 when Queen Elizabeth's reign began. She sponsored Drake and other seafarers. So began the establishment of what would become, 200 years later, the British Empire.

Did You Know?

Philip II ruled the Roman Catholic Spanish empire, the largest in the world at the time. After he married Queen Mary I of England in 1554, he also ruled England with her until her death in 1558.

The City of London
In the sixteenth century, London was the center of English trade and politics. It was home to a large, mostly poor population.

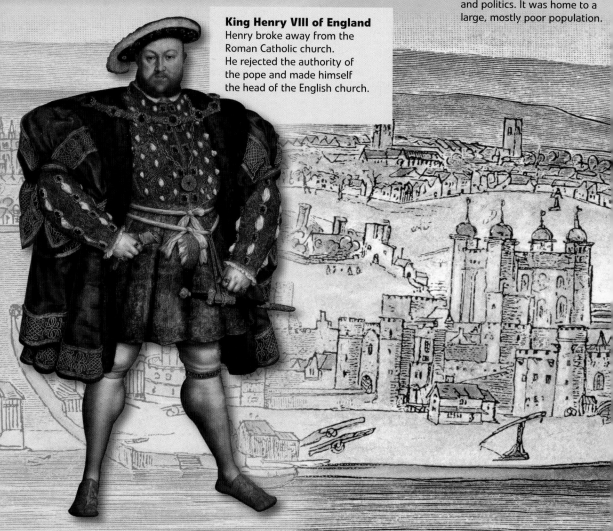

King Henry VIII of England
Henry broke away from the Roman Catholic church. He rejected the authority of the pope and made himself the head of the English church.

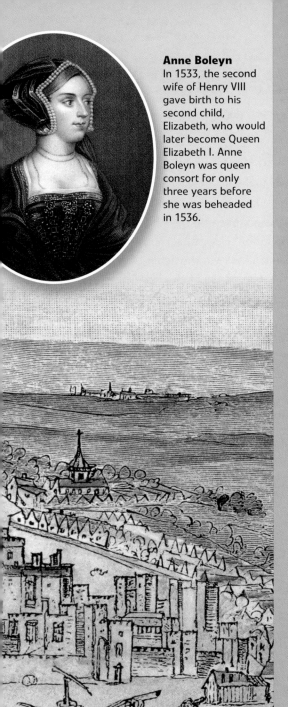

Anne Boleyn
In 1533, the second wife of Henry VIII gave birth to his second child, Elizabeth, who would later become Queen Elizabeth I. Anne Boleyn was queen consort for only three years before she was beheaded in 1536.

Difficult times

Queen Mary I was Henry VIII's first child. She ruled England from 1553 until 1558. Mary was a devout Roman Catholic, whereas many English people were Protestants. Her husband, Philip II, wanted England to join in a war against France. This was a time of religious persecution, civil unrest, and poverty.

Burned at the stake
Mary I reinstated the links with Rome and made the country Roman Catholic again. Several hundred people were burned at the stake for not becoming Roman Catholics or for refusing to give up their Protestant beliefs.

Rural life
Life was difficult for tenant farmers during the early Tudor period. However, it improved during Elizabeth I's reign.

Trade and Treasure

In 1519, the Portuguese explorer Ferdinand Magellan set out to search for a westward route to the famed Spice Islands. This voyage, once completed, became the first circumnavigation of the globe. Five ships rounded the bottom of South America via the Strait of Magellan, crossed the huge expanse of the Pacific Ocean, and successfully reached the Spice Islands (now the Moluccas of Indonesia). Most of the sailors on the voyage died en route, including Magellan, but some of the crew survived and made it back to Portugal.

This great voyage paved the way for Francis Drake, who followed a similar circumnavigation route almost 60 years later. During the intervening years, European countries fought to secure trade with Asia and plunder the wealth of the New World.

Silver and gold
The New World's precious metals were a source of vast wealth for Spain. Their colonies in South America provided labor for mining and refining the metals.

The Spice Islands
The Portuguese beat Spain to capture Melaka, the center of the spice trade and now part of Malaysia, in 1511. The two countries were fierce rivals for control of the trade. The Dutch and the English also wanted a share of it.

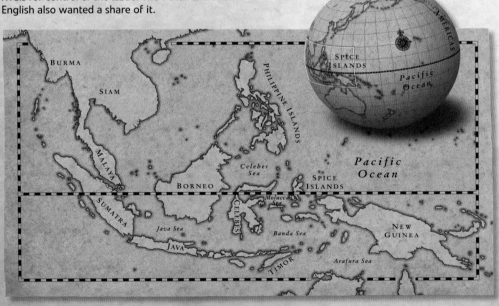

Inca treasures

The Spanish conquered the Inca people and occupied Peru during the sixteenth century. They stole many treasures of the Inca civilization from the capital, Cuzco. The Inca were renowned as craftsmen of fine gold and silver jewelry and precious artifacts.

Spice of life

Spices were valuable in Europe, with many more uses than simply flavoring food. Before refrigeration, spices were used to preserve food, improve spoiled food, and also to heal wounds and disease.

The Slave Trade

The English became aware of the riches of the New World and the Spaniards' use of African slave labor. John Hawkins—Francis Drake's second cousin—was a shipbuilder and merchant who, backed by wealthy English financiers, established a slave trading venture. Over seven years starting in 1560, Hawkins made three voyages from Plymouth. Drake accompanied Hawkins and in 1567, commanded his own vessel, *Judith.*

They raided Spanish slave ships and also kidnapped Africans from the west coast of Africa. They sold them as slaves at various ports in the West Indies. Hawkins, Drake, and the financiers all reaped financial rewards.

Transatlantic slave trade route
In the early to mid-sixteenth century, slaves were taken from West Africa to the West Indies. Later, Europeans shipped manufactured goods to West Africa, slaves to the Americas, and sugar and tobacco from the plantations back to Europe.

The trade
The Portuguese, who were later joined by the Spanish, began the trade in slaves. The strongest, healthiest Africans were most valued, and were sold at ports in the Americas to plantation and mine owners.

Ball and chain
Often, a solid iron ball was attached by a heavy chain to a slave's leg, or both legs were shackled together with a heavy chain. This was to stop slaves from jumping overboard or running away.

Cane cutter
The Spanish established large sugar
plantations in the West Indies. African
slaves were branded by their owners and
worked from sunrise to sunset. Cutting
and bundling cane was backbreaking
work in the heat. Slaves were also used
to mine gold and silver in Peru, working
in dangerous conditions.

The New World

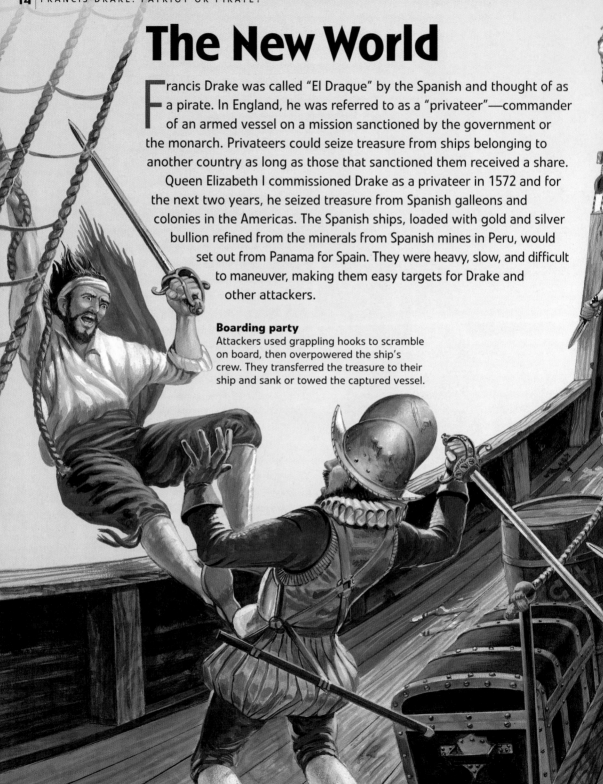

Francis Drake was called "El Draque" by the Spanish and thought of as a pirate. In England, he was referred to as a "privateer"—commander of an armed vessel on a mission sanctioned by the government or the monarch. Privateers could seize treasure from ships belonging to another country as long as those that sanctioned them received a share.

Queen Elizabeth I commissioned Drake as a privateer in 1572 and for the next two years, he seized treasure from Spanish galleons and colonies in the Americas. The Spanish ships, loaded with gold and silver bullion refined from the minerals from Spanish mines in Peru, would set out from Panama for Spain. They were heavy, slow, and difficult to maneuver, making them easy targets for Drake and other attackers.

Boarding party
Attackers used grappling hooks to scramble on board, then overpowered the ship's crew. They transferred the treasure to their ship and sank or towed the captured vessel.

Turbulence and treasure

The impact of Europeans on the indigenous peoples was disastrous. They had no resistance to the diseases the invaders brought with them. Those who survived illness were forced into slavery in their conquerors' mines.

Mining at Potosí, Bolivia
Potosí was established as a silver mining town in 1546. Indigenous laborers worked in slave conditions to extract the silver ore from nearby "rich mountain" and refine it.

Huguenots at Fort Caroline, Florida
French Huguenots were Protestants. A group of about 200 Huguenots fled France and settled in Fort Caroline, Florida, in 1564. The Spanish killed or imprisoned all the residents of the colony in 1565.

In the Americas

Francis Drake left Plymouth, England, in December 1577, with five ships. His instructions were to sail into the Pacific Ocean via the Strait of Magellan and investigate the extent of Spain's colonization along the west coast of the Americas. After the Strait, only Drake's ship, the *Pelican*, was fit to continue into the Pacific.

Drake renamed his ship the *Golden Hind* and sailed northward, pillaging Spanish settlements. He charted the unknown west coast of North America and completed the first leg of his great journey.

Attack at sea
In early 1579, Drake and crew attacked and boarded the Spanish treasure ship the *Nuestra Señora de la Concepción,* then overpowered the surprised Spaniards and unloaded the ship's full consignment of treasure.

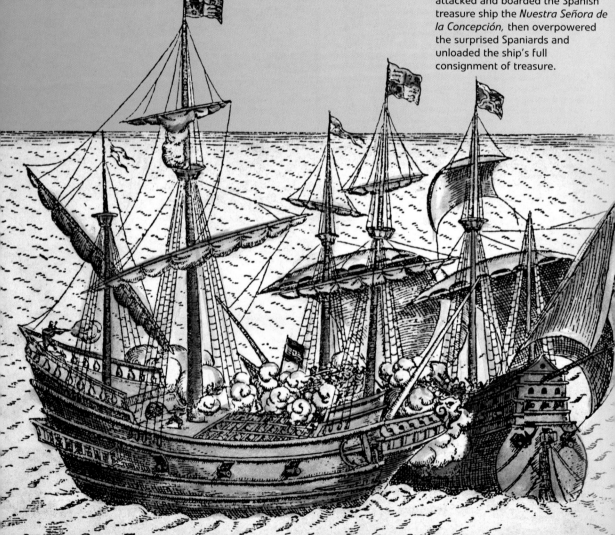

Landing in California

As he traveled up the American west coast, Drake landed in California, north of the northernmost Spanish settlement at Point Loma (in modern-day San Diego). He named the landing site Nova Albion and claimed the region for England.

Exploring the Americas

After landing in present-day California and considering the situation, Francis Drake decided to set sail for home across the Pacific Ocean. The *Golden Hind* was made ready for the historic second stage of its voyage of exploration.

Circumnavigation

No one is sure whether Francis Drake intended to circumnavigate the globe when he set sail from England in 1577. Perhaps he himself did not know, or perhaps the idea was kept secret. His convoy of five ships was armed to take on Spanish rivals. But with a full load of treasure on the *Golden Hind,* his decision to sail westward across the Pacific Ocean and toward the Spice Islands may have been influenced by his desire to avoid Spanish galleons.

Drake's Pacific Ocean crossing was assisted by easterly trade winds, but it still took more than two months. He spent time in the Spice Islands, then sailed around the Cape of Good Hope to return to a hero's welcome in England in September 1580.

Spices for England
The Portuguese, Spanish, and Venetians had better access to the spice trade than the English. In 1579, Drake obtained direct access to spices for England, and 21 years later the English East India Company was set up.

Sultan to the rescue
Drake arrived in Ternate, in the Moluccas, in November 1579 and stayed for almost two months. The Sultan of Ternate was welcoming and instructed his sailors to tow the *Golden Hind* into and out of Ternate harbor to ensure its safe passage.

Hidden reef
The *Golden Hind* was sailing for the island of Java and then home in 1580 when it grounded on a reef. Neither trying to tow the vessel nor removing some cargo to lighten it could set it free. Luckily, a sudden gale blew it clear the next day.

Celebes
Sea

*Pacific
Ocean*

MOLUCCAS

BORNEO

Molucca
Sea

CELEBES

Banda Sea

Java Sea

JAVA

Arafura Sea

Voyage of circumnavigation

Francis Drake completed his circumnavigation of the globe
almost 60 years after the first such voyage by Magellan.
Drake was the first Englishman to do it.

Island of Ternate

The dominant "spice island" nation was ruled by the powerful
Sultan of Ternate. When trade negotiations with the Dutch
broke down, the Sultan was happy to deal with Drake.

The *Golden Hind*

Galleons
Galleons were an important type of square-rigged sailing ship for seafaring nations such as Spain and England. They had three or more masts and decks.

The *Golden Hind* is famous as the ship that Francis Drake sailed around the world. It was a small galleon, about 70 feet (21 m) long and 20 feet (6 m) wide. It was originally called the *Pelican*, but Drake renamed it in 1578 in honor of Sir Christopher Hatton, one of the principal patrons of the voyage of 1577–1580. A hind (a female deer) was featured on the Hatton family crest.

Drake's circumnavigation was a feat of extraordinary seamanship and courage. The ship was considered of national importance after Drake's return, so it was dry-docked and put on public display, never to sail again.

Typical features

The *Golden Hind* may have possessed features similar to the galleon shown here. Two replicas of the ship still exist in England.

Sails
Square sails of tough canvas were hung from long spars, called yards, made from pine trees.

Bowsprit
Sails on the foremast were adjusted by lines attached to the bowsprit.

Life at sea
Life below decks was cramped and unhealthy. The crew shared their quarters with food supplies and rats attracted by the food. Officers would generally be in cabins on the upper decks.

Jib
The foremost sail, in front of the galleon's bow, was called the jib.

Lower decks
Livestock such as chickens were kept onboard to supply eggs and fresh meat. Other provisions included salted meat and drinking water.

Keel
The keel is the backbone of the ship; it runs from bow to stern. Galleon keels were made of seasoned oak or mahogany.

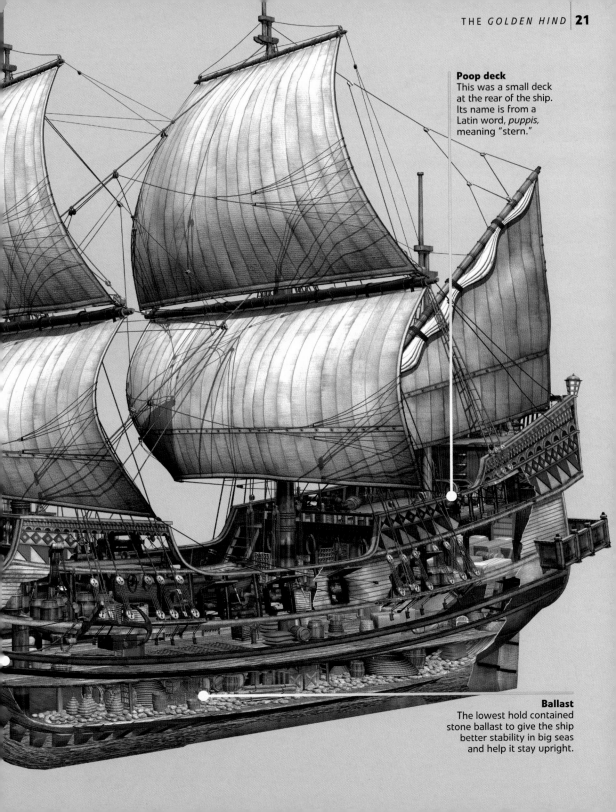

Poop deck
This was a small deck at the rear of the ship. Its name is from a Latin word, *puppis*, meaning "stern."

Ballast
The lowest hold contained stone ballast to give the ship better stability in big seas and help it stay upright.

Important People

Francis Drake was assisted by important people during his extraordinary life. The most significant was Queen Elizabeth I, who dedicated herself to making England a leader in world trade and exploration.

John Hawkins helped his second cousin Drake rise to fame and fortune. The two men led quite similar lives. Both commanded ships in England's victorious sea battle against the Spanish Armada, and both died of illness in the West Indies: Drake in January 1596, two months after Hawkins.

Sir Walter Raleigh

Sir Walter Raleigh was a distant relative of Drake. He set up a colony at Roanoke Island in North America in 1585. Raleigh's ship, the *Ark Royal*, was the flagship against the Spanish Armada.

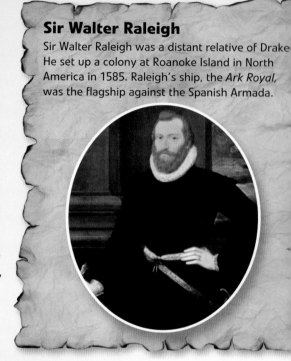

A gift of pearls

Queen Elizabeth I was grateful to Francis Drake and rewarded him. She encouraged his trading and exploration activities around the world and shared in the spoils that he brought home.

Sir John Hawkins

Sir John Hawkins (right) taught Drake (center) navigation and sailing. His family's wealth and his skills in seafaring and shipbuilding led, in 1578, to his appointment as Treasurer of the Royal Navy.

Sir Francis Walsingham

Walsingham was born into an aristocratic family. He rose quickly to become Queen Elizabeth's adviser on foreign policy. He was Drake's main financial backer but thought of him as a pirate.

King Philip II

The King of Spain tried to make England and Spain allies by marrying Queen Mary I of England, Elizabeth's older half-sister. However, the two countries became embroiled in war in 1585.

Ferdinand Magellan

This Portuguese-born explorer sailed under the orders of the Spanish king, Charles I. Between 1519 and 1521 he found a westward route from Europe to the Spice Islands. His exploits inspired Francis Drake.

Sir Francis Drake
Queen Elizabeth I knighted Francis Drake on the deck of the *Golden Hind* in April 1581. This was in recognition of his voyage around the world and the glory it brought England.

Fame, Wealth, and Plunder

To the rescue
Roanoke Island was an English colony set up in North America in 1585. When supplies ran short, Drake rescued the 100 colonists and sailed them back home to England.

Still the privateer
Francis Drake resumed his career as a privateer. The *São Felipe* was boarded off the coast of Portugal and its treasure taken. Spanish navy supply ships were attacked.

Francis Drake was knighted in 1581 and retired from the sea for a time. But, in 1585, he set out in a convoy of more than 25 vessels, bound for the West Indies, to plunder Spanish towns and settlements. Towns from the Cape Verde Islands to Florida were attacked, plundered, and destroyed.

Meanwhile, English spies gathered information that the Spanish were building up their navy in preparation for an attack on England. In April 1587, Drake took the Spanish completely by surprise, entering Cádiz harbor and destroying around 30 moored ships in 50 hours. The English suffered very minor damage by comparison. The damage to Spanish shipping delayed their planned naval attack on England by up to 12 months.

Cannon attack

The English warship *Vanguard* was one of about 25 new "race ships" that were designed by John Hawkins and Francis Drake. It was fast, could turn quickly, and its cannons, used at close quarters, penetrated the hulls of Spanish galleons below the waterline.

The Spanish Armada

King Philip II of Spain planned to wage war on England. The task of the Spanish Armada was to defeat the English Royal Navy. This would allow the Spanish army to cross the English Channel and overrun England. The Armada consisted of about 160 ships, manned by about 8,000 sailors, and carrying almost 20,000 soldiers. Many of these vessels were bulky and slow. The English fleet numbered about 200 more nimble ships. Drake was one of the leading commanders.

In July 1588, the Armada arrived off the English coast and anchored overnight in tight formation. The English sent eight fire ships toward the Spanish ships, forcing them to cut anchor and scatter. In the fiercely fought Battle of Gravelines, England won a great naval victory.

Destruction of the Armada
The remaining vessels of the Armada sailed north around the top of Scotland, then down the west coast of Ireland. Without good navigational charts and often without anchors, many were wrecked in storms. Fewer than half the ships and only about 10,000 men made it back to Spain.

?... You Decide

Most observers agree that Francis Drake was effective at achieving what he set out to do. But most people today would consider his methods savage and contrary to international law.

If there can be a justification for his actions, it is that he met violence with violence. He had an adventurous spirit, far-sightedness, perseverance, and above all, courage.

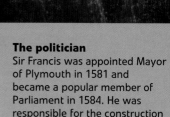

The *Golden Hind*
The galleon in which Drake circumnavigated the world was on public display for 100 years.

The politician
Sir Francis was appointed Mayor of Plymouth in 1581 and became a popular member of Parliament in 1584. He was responsible for the construction of Plymouth's water supply.

The statue
A 10-foot-(3 m) high bronze statue of Sir Francis Drake was unveiled in 1884, overlooking Plymouth Sound, England.

Raids on land
Drake also targeted treasure stores held in Spanish colonies throughout the New World, awaiting shipment to Spain.

Patriot

Drake, a commoner and daring sea captain, became Vice Admiral of the Royal Navy, a knight, and a hero to the people of England.

Pirate

The Protestant Drake was an opponent of Catholicism and Spain. He believed stealing from the Spanish was correct behavior.

Victory
The Admiral of the Spanish Armada surrendered to Sir Francis Drake, who acted as the representative of the English Royal Navy.

Leap from misery
Drake was a slave trader. Some African captives would leap off slave ships. They preferred death to bondage and misery.

Attack at sea
Spanish galleons, loaded with treasure and headed for Spain, were easy targets for Drake and other English privateers in their fast, maneuverable ships.

Gold
The Spanish considered Francis Drake a pirate and King Philip II reportedly offered a reward equal to $20 million for his capture.

Glossary

allies (A-lyz) Nations that are friendly with each other.

aristocratic (uh-ris-tuh-KRA-tik) Describes privileged members of a community, holding hereditary titles.

Armada (ar-MAH-duh) A fleet of armed ships, particularly referring to the Spanish navy.

artifacts (AR-tih-fakts) Objects made by humans, rather than by nature.

bondage (BAHN-dihj) The state of being under the control of, or a slave to, other people.

bow (BOW) The front part of a ship.

branded (BRAND-ed) Marked with a symbol burned into the skin with a special piece of red-hot metal.

bullion (BUL-yin) Thick bars of solid, precious metal.

circumnavigate (SER-kem-NA-vuh-gayt) To sail completely around something, especially the globe.

colonies (KAH-luh-neez) Specific areas in the world politically controlled by other countries.

consort (KAHN-sort) The wife or husband of a reigning king or queen.

dry-docked (DRY-dokt) Secured in a large dock from which the water has been removed.

dynasty (DY-nas-tee) A succession of sovereign rulers in the same family line.

dysentery (DIH-sun-ter-ee) A severe, sometimes fatal, infection of the digestive system.

embroiled (em-BROY-uld) Forced into a course of action or situation.

fire ships (FYR SHIPS) Ships burning intentionally, in order to spread fire to other ships.

foreign policy (FOR-in PAH-lih-see) The policy of a government that directs its relationships with other countries.

grappling hooks (GRAP-ling HUKS) Metal tools with several hooks at one end, thrown by a rope attached to the other end.

hulls (HULZ) The main bodies of ships.

Inca (ING-kuh) The group of people who originally lived in the Cuzco valley in Peru.

indigenous (in-DIH-jeh-nus) Born in and living in a particular place.

knight (NYT) A man on whom the English monarch, or ruler, has bestowed an honor in the form of military rank, in return for which the knight promises to serve the monarch.

maneuverable (muh-NOO-ver-uh-bul) Able to change position easily.

moored (MOORD) Secured at dock or to a mooring with ropes or cables.

nimble (NIM-bul) Able to turn and move quickly.

e (OR) Mineral rock that
ntains a valuable metal.

llaging (PIH-lihj-ing)
aling valuable goods,
ng violence.

antation (plan-TAY-shun)
arge area of land on which
nts or trees are grown.

litical alliance
h-LIH-tih-kul uh-LY-unts)
ond or treaty between nations
 mutual advantage.

otestant (PRAH-tes-tunts)
hristian religion that follows
 Bible as the only source of
ealed truth and rejects the
hority of the pope.

fining
-FYN-ing) Separating a pure
tal from the mineral rock
ich is mined.

religious persecution
(rih-LIH-jus per-sih-KYOO-shun)
Punishment dealt out to
people solely because of
their religious beliefs.

replicas (REH-plih-kuhz)
Copies of the original.

Roman Catholic
(ROH-mun KATH-lik) A Christian
religion led by the pope and
based in the Vatican.

seafaring (SEE-fer-ing)
Working in the business of ocean
sailing or shipbuilding.

spoils (SPOY-ulz) Goods or
property taken by force.

trade winds (TRAYD WINDZ)
Winds that blow steadily
across the ocean near
the equator.

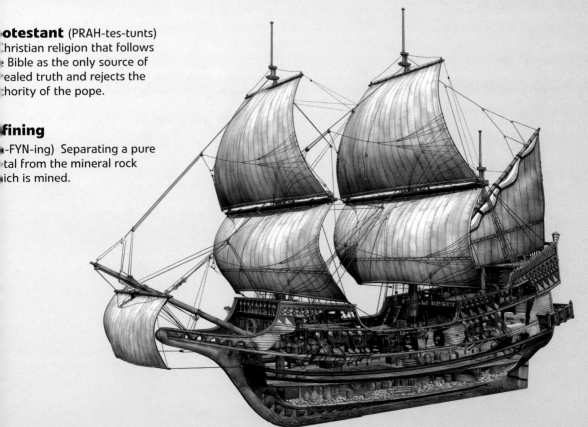

Index

Websites

Due to the changing nature of Internet links, PowerKids Press has developed an online list of websites related to the subject of this book. This site is updated regularly. Please use this link to access the list:
www.powerkidslinks.com/disc/drake/